The Esai Poems

Also By Jimmy Santiago Baca

BREAKING BREAD WITH THE DARKNESS

BOOK 1

The Esai Poems

by Jimmy Santiago Baca

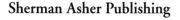

Sherman Asher Publishing   •   Santa Fe

ISBN: 978-1-890932-39-8

Library of Congress Control Number: 2011902001

Cover drawing by James Drake
Book designed by Jim Mafchir

Sherman Asher Publishing
126 Candelario St.
Santa Fe, NM 87501
www.shermanasher.com

Manufactured in the U.S.A.

To my family.

CONTENTS

HOLDING UP A MIRROR

Foreword by Carolyn Forché

FOR YEARS I HAVE BEEN GATHERING THE WORK OF POETS who have endured conditions of extremity in the brutal twentieth and twenty-first centuries—poets who suffered especially the brutalities of imprisonment, and survived to write of spiritual and physical wounds. Among them is Nazim Hikmet of Turkey, who spent half his adult life in prison, and whose writing is so suffused with its deprivations and agonies that even his poems about the late spring thaw of ice on a water jug suggest to his readers that this is a prison poem, written by a hand confined. Poets such as Nazim Hikmet wrote from all countries. The language of Nazim Hikmet, Paul Celan, Joseph Brodsky, Alexander Wat, Otto René Castillo and a host of others whose language has passed through the horrors of extreme experience to be indelibly marked. Jimmy Santiago Baca is their brother.

If the great historian Howard Zinn gave us the true history of our country, the peoples' history, then Jimmy Santiago Baca gives us its secret and present, and yes, dangerous reality: at the heart of our democracy, more people are imprisoned in the United States than anywhere else in the world. We have constructed an archipelago of industrial human warehouses, the brutalities of which include beatings and the torture of solitary confinement, that Jimmy Santiago Baca himself endured, as well as state-sanctioned and state-inflicted murder. This is the universe of the carceral imagination, and far, we are told, from where poetry flourishes. Yet Jimmy Santiago Baca not only wrote his first poems from the depths of solitary confinement, but he managed, with the help of a few books and a precious dictionary, to assemble the puzzle of literacy for himself, and so wrote his way to survival. His prose and poetry do more than give voice to his indomitable spirit; they take us on a perilous journey through bowels of our country. They also hold up a mirror—the kind convicts hold through the bars of their cells to see who is coming down the tier— a mirror held up to America that one hopes is not held up in vain or held up too late.

Jimmy Santiago Baca is an Indio-Chicano poet of New Mexico who has written some of the most lyrically beautiful images I have encountered concerning the sacredness of its mountains and llanos, arroyos and lakes. Listen to the music here:

> *wings of bees wedge board bin crack*
> *sticky with chile mash, and flies gorge*
> *in tin pails and buzz in paper sacks.*

And this about felling a tree:

> *Where the tree had stood*
> *a silver waterfall of sky now poured down.*
> *Still air. Red dusk. I felt I had just killed*
> *an old man.*

As compellingly as he writes of imprisonment, he writes of

childhood—his own and his children's—of his people: chicanos, Native Americans, farmers and laborers, and of the land, birds and animals. In many of his poems I hear Walt Whitman's spirit, and also Baca's poetic mentor, Pablo Neruda. Here is that spirit singing of America:

> *It's all well, husky barrel chested cities*
> *of America. Drowning in your liquor and gambling and*
> > *clothe*
> *your rebels and libraries, your blood vessels filled and gorged*
> *as if dams broke loose and hurtled toward gutters and*
> *gulches, none can stop you, all rush to their boats made*
> > *of bone,*
> *and sails made of red cloth from the heart, and sail you America,*
> *waving to others, all passing, passing and floating by.*
> *So in all your grand wonder and greatness, I wonder who*
> > *am I here?*

This is the question he asks America on our behalf. Jimmy Santiago Baca, who wrote his way back from a childhood of abandonment, orphanages, and detention centers, from a young manhood of confinement, who saw in literature a river that might bear him away, who became a poet, a memoirist, an essayist, a filmmaker and, most recently, a novelist, celebrates an important anniversary. After spending twenty-five years in prison, he has now spent twenty-five years, a free man who—has been for a longer time free than confined. He is a man free in many senses of the word but most importantly, free in the word that gives strength and hope to others.

In *Breaking Bread with the Darkness: Book One, The Esai Poems*, we hear a voicing of that hope.

Here, Baca addresses his son, Esai, as a newborn, commending to him a great measure of love and wisdom. How many poets have written so unabashedly to those who have just entered the world, or kept poetic vigil with such tender precision without forgetting the world about him:

> *The day Saddam Hussein was captured*
> *president Bush bestowed billion-dollar kickback contracts*
> *to CEO mobsters in the oil racket*
> *to build cities he ordered bombed.*

This, too, is the world young Esai has entered, along with

> *licked pears,* and *mango juice* and *phonetic babbles,* a father
> shouting through the foliage your new name,
> *Boogadoo! Boogadoo!*

Breaking Bread with the Darkness is a primer for paternity, a poetic model for teaching the young history, politics, spirituality and survival, introducing the new generaton to an alphabet soup of another sort, where SWAT, CNN, MIA, and so on swirl about us. Jimmy Santiago Baca, the father and poet, has written a rare book for the new generation. This book describes the world as it is, and is rarely described. This is poetry taking all the right chances for all the right reasons in a very precarious time. A poetry of intelligence, judgement, and love was never more necessary.

A mi hermano en la lucha,

Carolyn Forché
February, 2011

PREFACE

25 In/25 Out

THE REASON I WROTE THE ESAI POEMS and the other three books that will follow, was to celebrate my children, celebrate taking steps in any direction I wanted, to open any door, to greet the morning sun with prayers and a smile, to plan my day as freely and exhilaratingly as a trapeze artist soaring through the air with no net nor anyone to catch me. And now, it's sort of my anniversary. It is my anniversary. From the age of five to thirty-one I was in the system: from St. Anthony's Orphanage, to the Detention Center, to Montessa the Gladiator School for adolescents heading to prison, to the Bernalillo County Jail, and finally to Arizona Maximum Security prison in Florence, Arizona. Twenty-five years in the system, brutal, corrupt, hate-filled, and frenzied with violence. The system. And somehow I managed to get out alive, but not without deep emotional scars and spiritual wounds that continue to haunt me to this day: beatings, shock-therapy, abandonment, terror, death threats, stabbings—I was shot, stomped on, homeless and living on the streets, unschooled, and illiterate.

I did it. To all of the above horrors I say: I have outlasted you. This September 2010 marks the time that I have been more free than imprisoned; twenty-five years in the system, twenty-five years and one month out in freedom. Working strong and standing with integrity and writing and loving and with family and five kids and every morning, I mean, every single morning, I rise I do so with gratitude and love for my breath, for stepping into the kitchen, for tossing up my four-year-old Lucia, for riding bikes with my seven-year-old Esai, for looking out the window and seeing the vast blue sky, and for hugging my wife and running around the fields or up in the foothills. I so, so love life.

And I know that people rarely enjoy every moment with unconscionable joy. But I do. Every moment my heart is a tambourine and my exhalations are the brown hands of a freed man beating his freedom calls, his own clarion roostering, dawn-awaking cry that life is good, life is amazing with friends and food and parks and children and poetry and writing and books! Joy my brother, joy my sister, is what my soul clangs as if it were one of those huge bronze drumheads in front of a Buddhist temple and I gong it gong it gong it with love for life!

And then sometimes I have had to seclude myself and express my joy in words, on these pages, these four books, these poems to my children. I also write about experiences that shaped me, molded my thinking, shaped my soul into a vase that serves to hold each dawn like lilacs. These four books contain my experiences; my poems mourn, celebrate, dance, reach out to embrace the world, test the water of national issues, confront bigotry, and always, always dive from the highest peaks into the churning waters of contemporary turmoil in education, prison-reform, sex, war, love, and more.

Enough, let's read!

JSB September 2010

PROLOGUE

Esai, ever since I can remember
you loved stones and lizards and water and trees and wind—
      your small legs were the fingers of a piano man
      lulling the world with an elegy,
         the fingers on black stones and white winged grasshoppers
         ringing sweetest regrets and frailness,
the tenderness of a slight breeze that strums a dandelion stem,
      I see sadness in it,
I see myself in you, your brown eyes brightening to the sudden scurry
of a lizard from a tumbleweed,
      "Look! Papa!"
and I do, the memory of your laughter this afternoon;
your hand clutching mine so we won't get lost.

      Esai, Esai, Esai,
      play the black and white hours in your adventure
      to journey down each day, sometimes weeping,
sometimes laughing,
let your beautiful feet rush through the grass as if each
                          blade of grass
were a harp string

and you are falling from string to string, a tiny little fellow
reduced to the size of a lizard,
       and my goodness, play the songs of giants my son,
as if the whole world were present in our living room,
all of us sitting on boulders and in trees and next to creeks,
       climb my sweet son and follow the lizards
       across the red stones of your heart's landscape
       and offer the world a red laughter
       when you find a pebble that glows
       with the lizard's footprint
             that run across the soft red sand of your heart,
             along an unending ocean called your joy!

I love you sweet son,
and all around me each day like gray and blue and black and red
snowflakes
lizards are falling from the sky into the ocean
of your unending joy.

My song to you is this:
       snow fills the night, mounds and mounds of snow in the streets
       while street lamps like old Russian poets stare at the flakes and
ponder
       what the cold means, what the night means, what the flakes mean—
             and then far away someone in one of the lit
             windows of the many rooms
             starts to play a very soft and sad piano
             and beyond that, the ringing of a bell is heard,

and the street lamps glow brighter, the piano's

volume increases,

and through the snowy streets

you come ringing the bell to announce

I have lizards and stones, lizards and stones.

PART ONE

12-15-03

Esai collects dreams
in the nest of his palm
farm-sweet blackberry juice
stains his hands and lips.

Were he able to speak about the blackberries,
Esai would simply say God.

He wakes from his afternoon siesta,
flapping legs and hands,
a bluebird perched on the birch branch of mother's arm
                              ready to raid
                              cornfields
                              in his father's heart.

12-16-03

Esai watches
Bessie, short and stocky,
our eighty-four year old Greek neighbor
on her roof stringing Christmas bulbs at night.

Coastal shoulders,
left arm braced against her left knee,
in a peasant bundle coat and headscarf,
        she hunches down against the cold,
        determined to celebrate
        the birth of Baby Jesus.

The next morning,
Esai crawls along the edge of the kitchen,
stringing movements
his hands and knees create,
that flash bright in his mind
in the festive possibilities of all earthly infants,
from Jesus, Dalai Lama, Mother Theresa, Buddha, to Esai
star at the tip of the tree of life
one knee in front of the other, hands flat on floor,
        celebrating his first Christmas.

12-17-03

I remember when you found your nose,
a small, soft ornament
that itched and sneezed scaring you to tears;
and how happy you were to find
your hands,
two wonderful appendages with five
lovely fingers attached to them.

I wake up next to you,
in the semi-dark your head bobs above the blankets.
We smile at each other, friendly sailors
beached,
after surviving exotic ports and rowdy storms,
now find ourselves in the same bed,
in the same world, amazed at our bodies,
at our breath, flesh, at our wiggling toes,
and our ability to sit and see with our eyes—
amazing globes below our foreheads that can miraculously
observe the mysteries
of trees, birds, clouds, faces, morning light.

I cup palms around my mouth and murmur animal sounds—

you giggle, our voices echo throughout the house,
                you grunt
                        I warble
                        you lick your palm and taste your finger
                        I do too.

Your mama awakens
we snuggle into her breasts
you for milk, me her flesh
                you mutter comfortably
                                I growl lavishly deep chest hungering lust.

Your tiny hands massage her breasts
squeezing them like tortilla dough—
tiny hands
                that will have to fight for dignity,
                claw through and dig up
                struggling your way to peace,
                bloody knuckled, scratched and cut,
chapped from cold and work,
                will my sweet baby
                                find strings of an instrument
                                to play your song of life on,
                                strumming them to a music
                                of your own, as you grope and caress
                                the walls and floors and flesh of your dream
                                to express your heart—

ravage discrimination with your roar for equality,

voice your solitary opinion amidst the unruly mob,
avoid drugs, booze, liars, and hustlers,
be compassionate to the oppressed, befriend the homeless,
be one of those marching in the streets to defend your civil rights,
deliriously laugh, weep, embrace your family,
love life my son—

        as you discover your body now
        discover your immense spiritual power
            as you grow
                with as much amazement and thankfulness....

12-19-03

The day Saddam Hussein was captured
President Bush bestowed billion-dollar kickback contracts
to CEO mobsters in the oil racket
to rebuild cities he ordered bombed,
my woman was cutting my hair in the bathtub;
I was standing up naked while you sat on the bathroom floor, Esai,
gazing up at my penis, looking down at yours,
making all kinds of guttural sounds;
   after showering,
   we sat in your playroom,
   I sat on the footstool and slapped my penis
   against my thigh, you laughed,
   growled and I slapped my penis again and again
   until you fell backward laughing so hard
   the whole time grunting at me more to make me
   whack my penis
     against my inner thigh.
That's the kind of Americans we are,
     penis-whackers,
     not war-mongers.
We had fresh carrot juice, a fruit plate and coffee for breakfast,
we sat in bed and sucked orange wedges,

bit pineapple chunks,
chewed apples, licked pears, sipped mango juice.
The sunrise
spreading over the three of us
in bed in New Mexico,
nibbling fruit and kissing each other's fingers—
that's the kind of Americans we are.

12-20-03

Recently I showed you how to clap,
stand on two feet,
utter new sounds,
climb one step up and down
from kitchen to sunroom,
slap water and splash,
squeeze rubber ducks, frighten birds to see them scatter—
        then you teach me
        to snuggle, hug, kiss, and laugh,
        to give my heart to every moment of the day.

12-21-03

We communicate in bird calls and dog barks,
shriek excitement and leap
when we see each other.

I dance around you, lean low to kiss your head,
you erratically swirl
uttering a multitude of phonetic babbles
tongue-slavering joy for your existence.

We invent our language of love,
hilarious names for each other,
you humming my names,
me shouting like a huge
friendly bird in the foliage
your new name,
                          Boogadoo! Boogadoo!
And your reply ricochets in all the rooms
Yay, yah, yah!

12-22-03

The last few days Kim and I
have been cleaning out the garage,
stuff that belongs mostly to my oldest son
dumped in haphazard heaps last week
after moving out of his apartment.

Junk: CD cases, hip-hop clothes, dirty fish tank,
plastic planter buckets, exercise bicycle
he used after his ACL operation
                    and all kinds of other rubbish.

I don't like cleaning up people's trash,
after they sit around all day and party,
leave the house filthy,
refrigerator moldering green inside
with rotten food, carpets littered
with cigar ash and tobacco, hamburger wrappers
paper cups—
                    but like a good parent
                    hoping to get back my damage deposit
                    I go over and vacuum and sweep up as well
                    as I can,

which doesn't help, it's just too filthy
and I don't have the stomach or time to clean it up good.

As I drive home,
I think he better not mess my house up,
time he learned how to pick up after himself,
get a job, good grades in school, start making a life for himself.

All these things go through my head
            when the radio announces more GI's
            killed in Iraq—
            day after day young poor men
            being picked off, blown up,
            shot, bombed, mutilated, cannibalized—
            I vow—no matter how bad my son is at not
            arranging his life, he's not going
            to fall for those military commercials
            manipulating kids to join the armed services,
            dangling enticements of paid college tuition,
            flying jets, scuba diving
            or bouncing over rough terrain in Humvees—
            in truth, he'd be giving his life
            to brim the bank vaults for Bush's oil buddies,
            and it's not happening—
            my son does not have to prove his patriotism
            by sacrificing his life in a war so rich corporations
            can own more oil—
            murdering children and innocent men and women
            leaves a stain on the soul that won't clean off.

12-23-03

I understand a little more what's going on
as I get older,
I don't rely on TV or newspapers, they lie—
my own experience over the years has taught me
to see how things work now—
why powerful LA producers
censor Palestinian films,
Iraqi documentaries are banned
and why certain directors keep their lips sealed
and won't dare condemn the censure
fearful of being blacklisted.

The morning paper
describes how jail guards beat
three Chicanos last night.

My nine-month-old infant crawls on fours
room to room
and I imagine Iraqi children
in bombed debris and choking dust
crawl on fours over their murdered parents
as eighteen-year-old American soldiers

shoot them in the streets.
I used to plant trees during the year,
give away gifts for the giving,
invite friends to stay in my home,
volunteer to tutor illiterate adults,
        and than I stopped giving,
        withdrew, lost hope,
refused
to plant any trees,
                to share food with friends,
                declined to defend my convictions,
                to leave my house,
                to believe in peace.

But I can't live that way,
am surfacing gradually again,
abscessed molar
pulled out by pliers,
            withdrawing myself from the painful silence,
            to listen to the gunshots again
            and follow their source,
            to face the faces and stare into the eyes
            again of those CEOs
            stockpiling money and weapons, barricaded in
            by powerful thugs wearing police uniforms.

I am finally strong enough to go to the spot
where police murdered a stranger last December,
I kneel on the asphalt to touch his blood stains.

33 ✳

I remember how he smiled when he peeled past pedestrians
in his wheelchair, until that day
    when he refused to take his depression medication,
    refused to blur his brain with pills,
    and saw how violent the world was
    and wheeled himself out into the street and cried at people
    to come to their senses—
    they shot him.

His mother gives away his clothes
to homeless laborers she hires to clean her yard;
shirts, pants and shoes the homeless now wear
as they stand in cold lines downtown
shivering to get a hot meal.

12-24-03

The priests tell me I sabotage the Bible's teaching
by insisting the Church does not do enough for the poor.
Black councilmen tell a national talk-show host
that blacks are the only legitimate minority in America—
wealthy philanthropists cozy before fires
in Santa Fe mansions,
drink eggnog and rum, cognac and wine,
fur coats rot, diamonds brim jewel boxes,
morning frost gleams on their barbwire and alarmed walls,
nestled before TVs watching
brown-skinned peoples labeled targets,
watch slaughtering of children and women
called, Operation Santa claws,
words blurt out—attack, raids, roadblock, lethal gas,
guerillas, weapons, confiscation, Bradley armored vehicles, tanks,
blasted open,

> and these rich people feel safe,
> see faces of famished eyes
> behind jail bars staring out at them,
> as they sip their drinks,
>
> > feeling safe.

12-25-03

In the sunroom my son cries out
happiness at sunlight strobes slanting through the big windows
and spreading over his face;
> the sun has caught him
> in its bright net,
> and weaves his laughter in its
> golden design.
It's a game he and the sun play
each morning,
two infants playing tag in the school yard of life,
chasing after each other, rolling on the floor,
climbing the walls.

> The sun acknowledges his existence,
> welcomes him each morning
> at the door, offering flowers and birds
> and warmth.
How is it, that
the Census Bureau claims my son does not exist?
How is it racists say he is an illegal alien?
How is it society accuses him of taking their jobs?
Police profile him as a drug dealer?

And since Chicanos have a high number of deaths in every war,
Generals at the pentagon
believe Chicanos are suicidal, having nothing to live for
except to sacrifice his life in their war.

The wealthy look at me as a tireless gardener
and housekeeper, someone to raise and feed their children,
wash their dishes, sweep their floors,
seldom speak, scrub their toilets—
            Esais are everywhere,
            in the streets, on every corner,
            look out the window, you will see
            sixty-million Esais the government claims do not exist;
                        yet, know the time will come,
                                    when Esai cannot tolerate the injustices
                                                anymore,
                        and the newspapers, TVs,
Police and FBI will label him insurgent,
sunlight accompanying his every step....

12-26-03

Esai in bed
between his mother and me,
arms extended up at the dark ceiling.
He studies his hands as if they are newly discovered planets,
rotates them slowly, radiant swans
gliding over the silence of pre-dawn
in our bedroom,
causing airy ripples of light waves.
      It's Christmas season,
        but I won't celebrate this year—
        no tree up, no presents, won't send any cards;
        too many wars, too many lies from politicians,
        too much hatred and racism and indifference,
        too many people arguing they are right,
        too many wrecked kids in the streets,
        too many indifferent parents,
        too many obsessed with making more money,
        too many on drugs because they need it
        to survive and endure the numbing madness
        of a world that can kill all day and sleep so peaceful at night,
        of a world of people who's goal is to control the universe,
            to amass power at any expense, to manufacture bombs

to annihilate millions of people at once—so no
I will not
string Christmas lights in the yard
and pretend for appearance
that this Christmas is fine—
it is not.

The darkness of my yard announces to passersby
my brooding disillusionment.
I skulk search an answer to ease my melancholy mind,
but I know I can't escape
my sadness with books of poetry, hiking trails, bicycling
or visiting friends—
I must indulge my sadness,
sit in my room, count each and every penny of sadness,
engraved with the endless faces of murdered Palestinian children,
Israeli women blown to bits, Afghani and Iraqi citizens
buried under tons of blasted concrete.
But my coins are worthless,
they have no value other than to allow me
to grieve
for those people who are not here to share
this Christmas with their loved ones.

12-26-03

Watching my baby play with his hands in the dark,
warble ooings
immersed in the mystery of his own presence,
    how hands, tiny ones, could be so beautiful
    and amazing,
he marvels at their texture, dexterity, length, and width—

    I'll wait to tell him how in some places
    armies cut off the hands of rebels,
    how hands in Palestine, instead of touching
    loved ones and held by loving mothers,
    tie red and blue wires to a bomb to their chest,
    and that other hands sign official papers
    in Washington, DC, to execute a hundred-thousand
    innocent civilians;
    in some places the dawn
    is not as quiet nor as sweet as ours nor as loving
    with his mother and I beside him—
        blood runs brimming the gutters
        in Guatemala, in Chile
        cut-off heads glare at pedestrians from bushes,
        in the Gaza strip and West Bank

women's hands and legs
dangle from tree limbs,
in Ecuador, Peru, Bolivia, Mexico,
and many other places
poor people are herded out of their homes at night,
murdered and buried in mass graves.

I will tell my son only
that

when I was young,
I used to form my hands into animals shapes
projected profiles of bird figures against a wall
a dog was barking, a horse rearing.

How that innocent children's game came in handy
when I was older and sent to prison,
and, forbidden to speak,
I had to shape my hands into words
to convey a message to a prisoner in another cell,

not allowed to talk,

I signaled my speech to others,
And even when they threw me in an isolation cell
with only a peep hole to peek through,
when I spied another eye's pupil across the tier
staring at me,

I learned to communicate with my pupil—
I'll tell my son
that there is
a language of the oppressed,
and I know how to speak it well.

12-27-03

I am scared to be me
in an America where poets
fear imprisonment for
saying the wrong things,
where so many Hispanic writers and poets
drone the harmless verses
in mindless servitude
to prove they are patriotic Americans,
tout they are authentic citizens,
dummying up and modeling
as tame Black, Latino and Indian writers
on talk shows and radios,
repeating the President's liturgy
that war is necessary.

12-28-03

My gift to the world
is Esai, his hands
in the semi-dark move into their own
interpretations of life, love, compassion,
fingers wiggle like worms in garden soil,
             performing magic,
                    a sorcerer with wand
                           making an ordinary dawn
                           special;
      he intently focuses on his fingers' movements
      one finger up and down, then all five spread, then his
      whole hand
      arched down in swan neck fashion,
      his left hand joins his right in this dance
      honoring the dawn,
      dark silhouettes contrast against the window
      where the day with its trees, mountains, and housetops
             slowly become visible
             with more light to view them with,
             as the dark angel in his altar
             dances its coming, its life force,

43 ✻

beckoning it to come and scatter its seed-sparks,
its cold, chilled sparkles of light
brimming the old dented pails my heart is
with love

12-29-03

Esai wakes up, sits up
between his mother and I,
small person in the feather blanket,
fingers pulling at his toes,
eyes rove the room
meditate on the beige walls;
shadows cross the ceiling
surrendering to blue dawn,
the large windows facing north
suddenly unveil a startling view of the Sandia mountains,
clear as if they were created yesterday,
draws my son's rapt attention for a long time.

When I turn and smile at him,
he greets me with kindest, most tender smile
and I too am drawn out from my own darkness
into his delightful light, am created anew in his eyes,
believing in love and life more than ever.

Pope John Paul II urges the world
to peace during his Christmas mass,
Disney parades fill the streets

and football games roar on TV.
School break promises lots of kids
marijuana, heroin, snort and drink at all night parties.
Parents wake up with hangovers,
gift wrappings strewn over the floor
in every house except mine,
        deep down in my soul
            I don't know if I believe in God anymore,
    or in goodness
    as much as I did last year,
    I value people less and human life
              even less.

In bed next to me
my infant smiles and claps his hands,
marvels at the way he can rotate his arms
in circles at side,
and beyond him my blue-eyed sandy-haired woman
    sleepily opens her eyelids,
    and I realize I have nothing to compare
    this moment of happiness to—
    I feel,
        waking up knowing my other two sons are safe,
    that Gabe and Tones are loving men,
    that these are the gifts I've been blessed with
    speaking, feeling, thinking and loving human beings
    I am alive to enjoy and experience
        life here with them.
I sit up and mimic Esai,
clap and laugh,

Esai and I
clap and laugh on the bed, two monkeys
waking in a rain forest canopy,
thrilled to my hairy ass,
swinging from tree to tree, Esai and I,
our laughter a whole cluster of ripe bananas
in our beautiful make-believe tree
this morning is,
not a Christmas season morning
but a yellow banana morning
we peel back and eat.

12-29-03

My friends from Toronto and San Francisco
are getting up,
water pipes in this old house
shudder with life,
        groan their stretching bones
        as water rushes through rusty galvanized tunnels
        through the water heater downstairs in Gabe's room—
        under the shower nozzle, I splash my barrel-chest
        squat shoulders and muscled thighs,
        brick-shouldered from field working days,
        my face, hair and hands now dusted
        with Redi-Mix cement.
                        Water pearls
        onto my legs, arms, penis and hands
        my lips and cheeks tighten
        awakening to the cold morning,
        a chilly 21 degrees.
I make breakfast for my friends
the sun
mirror flashing flashes cornfield
across the blue sky, the frigid, clear landscape—

I compare this brilliance
to the smoke of 9/11,
the images of horrified people
hysterically dashing for safety,
their faces crusted in death dust
tears etched their cheeks—
what happened to our fairytale fable
of America that day?
That day, the swans in our minds were murdered,
that day the idyllic pond on which the swan floated
was polluted,
that day our out-going vigorous vibrancy for life
turned mean and savage as we looked for culprits to blame
for shattering our fairytale,
the one we need to believe in so much
that made our lives bearable

        that had us believing we were special,
        that had us blinded to anything beyond America's
        shores,
        that had us as characters in a fable
        where life was sweet and fulfilling and promised us
            everything tomorrow.
Suddenly the homeless men and women
burrowing in dumpsters for food
were dining on a swan meat,
suddenly millions of amputees from American bombs
were roasting swan meat,
suddenly, swan meat was all we had to eat that day.

This jeweled clarity of air
emerges with hope for the future,
the lies have burned away
with the mist,
and replaced with this blinding radiance of light
spreading through the pine and fur trees,
glinting at the snow peaked Sandias,
down through the South Valley,
across the frosted-stiff corrals
and crusty dog houses and frozen weeds;
we have endured it all, the light seems to say,
forgive ourselves, the light pleads.

On all fours
blazing his way forth
from room to room,
a strand of light
fleshed out, learns
to keep its glow glowing,
love contained in his smile, his laughter, his playfulness,
from time to time, unable to keep so much love subdued,
he roars and accidentally shakes the window panes loose from their
frames,
hair-line cracks appear over the tiled floors
and ceiling corners, creating
a slow crumbling of
this house, this morning, these friends
even my own life,
and in every room air gently flows

as a poet's verses whispered in a silent room,
and again, people shake off the dust of war
and slip on their scarves, gloves, hat and long coat,
shaking off the dust of war
with each step.

12-30-03

much of what I write,
the poems that is, are stones
I litter the dusty roads with
so kids can pick them up readily
to throw at tanks.
Much of what I write are like bullets
to reload the rifles of peoples
fighting for their land and their way of life.
Much of what I write
is my way of revealing to me
what CEOs want to conceal—
                    my words the black
                    blindfolds I cut loose
and when I do,
I find myself in basements, in strange places
I have never been,
and outside I hear
gunshots and children running
from dictators.

12-30-03

You stand up now
holding onto the cupboard handle or my hand.
                    Coming out of the burrow of blankets
                    sitting on your haunches
                    back straight as a squirrel,
you scan the bedroom,
left   right   down   up
then dive into me,
embracing my face, small arms and hands
feel so good on me,
                    then you robustly hug your mother
                    with the same bearish delight—
There is so much delight in you
so early,
so much relish for life radiates from your gestures,
so much faithfulness and confidence
in life's inherent goodness
not to harm your open heart and lovely soul,
you smile on each person you meet,
laugh as if laughter pollinated
plants to unfurl,
and all around us flowers blossom.

53 ✹

As if laughter were a way of making you
any animal you wanted, when you smiled
you the horse galloped through a meadow,
when you smiled you the sparrow
balanced on the branch outside
when you smile
you your soul
flies
like a sunrise over the landscape
touching all things equally with light.

12-31-03

The highchair
you sit in at breakfast
smearing applesauce all over your face
and gumming the apple slice
while the morning moves sideways like a giant blue lizard
past the windows
      its blue dinosaur feet
      suction cups at the windows.
      It pauses, its black tongue flicking,
                  flickering,
                  snatching up warm dreams.

1-04-04

Esai, celebrate your mixed blood—
Ibericos, Phoenicians, Celts, Visigoths, Romans, Moors,
Olmecs, Mayans, Toltecs, Aztecs, and Incas,
Seeds buried in your bone marrow
flourish a forest in your blood—
in the rainforest of your black hair
sacred quetzal birds caw,
and ancient origins of Indio/Arab/Jewish rivers
mix as they rush through you,
mimicking tears of one tribe, laughter of another,
in you a thousand lives celebrate and mourn,
your heart was the size of a pomegranate seed,

                                   quenched both
to rise up in rioting blossoms and fiercely
bow before the dawn's splendor:

        on hands and knees
        you scuttle around the house,
        growl like a jaguar,
        your brown-hazel eyes peek around the kitchen archway,
        flash behind the bedroom French doors,
        you scamper on all fours like a young prong-deer
        as I chase you, nonsense words giggle out from your throat

                    a flock of egrets
exploding across the living room,
swoop into the dormant fireplace, vanish up
the chimney toward the sky.
In the sunroom, sunlight pierces the shadows
quivering to reveal your jaguar jaws
clamped around a yellow rubber duck—
                    Tribal infant,
          you raise your arms to the sky,
          standing up against the couch,
          testing your stance, your balance shaky,
your small rose-leaf hands release from the couch
clap a thankfulness prayer,
your eyes dart at me
and I smile at you, now changed into a tawny fawn,
alert ears twitching for danger
before you incline your sleek neck and sip water
from the river of life running between us.

Later in the morning,
in the bathtub, about to cry, choking breath back,
almost-tears transform into a cough then change to a whine
and end up as laughter—

1-10-04

You shake me all up Esai,
the way you maneuver on all fours
racing through your playroom like the Roadrunner,
into our bedroom, swerving into the bathroom
and then heading out on the long trek into the kitchen
and finally after working your way down two steep steps
into the sunroom, you find us, standing up and clutching
the gray leather couch you show us how
you've been practicing to fall on your hands
rehearse your release and dive to the floor
cliff-diver from Acapulco
turn and catch yourself with your two palms flat on the floor
roll and laugh at us with as much enjoyment
as a Calvary-bugle charge;
confidently smile, you rise to explore the universe,
clinging to walls and falling on your butt
turning over on the floor, clapping,
squealing with delight, catching our gaze you erupt
with laughter, giggles, hiccups, and later at the store
buying lemons and apples in the produce section
an Asian woman
glances at you and you scrunch up your face
grinning, your whole face creased into a smile

as she gasp, 'Oh, thank you,' and folds her hands together
and nods in gratitude to your spirit passing hers
and giving her so much pleasure with your attentive welcome.

Esai, I get all shook up
at how much love you pour into the world,
your vocal sounds are Buddha bells ringing people to prayer,
to remind us we are sacred, our lives offerings for Gods,
that reclined in our cushioned, thorn-trimmed hearts,
angels, and ancestors await us—

I get all shook up thinking
about how much love you give the world daily, Esai,
all shook up when your eyes
minutely study the features on my face
your small hands run over my beard
your eyes fill with a certain look
as if we knew each other a long time ago,
met on the rough terrain of this mountain face of mine,
were both gold prospectors, you leading
a mule clanging with pots and pans and picks and shovels up a rocky
incline goat trail
and I was a small sparrow on the sage brush limb chirping
when you pause to pour a capful of water from your canteen
into a stone basin I sipped up thirstily,
                    quenching more than my thirst Esai.

1-19-04

War, Politics & Poetry

A few exceptional
poets and writers like Adrienne Rich,
Ferlinghetti, Chomsky, and Roy,
                    spoke out after 9/11
                    against pre-emptive strikes
                    in Afghanistan
                    and then later in Iraq.
Most of our high-profile writers
were silent,
as streets and buildings swarmed with police and military,
SWAT teams trooped up and down staircases, in and out of homes,
arresting brown-skinned peoples—
                    I saw them handcuffing hundreds
                    on CNN, young men and women
                    dragged off and shoved in police vans.
Holstered guns, shiny badges, lead-filled clubs, black buffed boots,
bullet-cartridge belts, mace and handcuffs
their bull necks craned, eyes hypnotized by replays
of two planes exploding into the Twin Towers,
                    then as if on a mission from God

terrorizing citizens
and few of the high-profile writers or poets
uttered a word of dissent.
It was not convenient for their careers.

When they noticed me standing at the bus stop,
the police cruiser stopped, the officers glared
with scorn, their law-enforcement eyes
suspecting me of crimes.

Feeling less American
with brown skin, black hair and brown eyes,
I quickly left, deciding to walk to my destination.

The words the poets and writers wrote on the pages
don't fit their obedient compliance
and I wonder why
so timid?
I feel a caution in the air,
uneasiness among writers
measuring their convictions
out in teaspoon doses,
celebrated before 9/11, now
MIA,
anxious about
being blacklisted,
their words
cooled to lukewarm, then
room temperature.

I read about them in the *Washington Post,*
New York and LA *Times,*

                    People or the *New Yorker,*
                    and they never speak up for the oppressed,

or against the war,
pleased at being patronized and pitied
as a wounded minority history has wronged,
wearing fine suits and dresses
on Oprah and Charlie Rose they stammer
as they confess

                    that they support
detainment without legal representation,
and pre-emptive strikes.

                  They were not alone—
                  celebrated actors and actresses,
                  astute intellectuals and movie directors,
cowered under kitchen tables in fear.

Suddenly,
those who had embraced mix-breed radicals
as tides to shores under a motherly moon,
under the glaring heat of patriotic fervor,
quoted scriptures, finger-licking
the sugary Popsicle of privilege.

Their conscious on trial,

                    purred for mercy
                    meowed furry lullabies

for hand-outs
from wealthy caressing hands
crooned nursery rhymes
endorsed by the weak-kneed fans.

&

I showed up in Mexico City to protest
World Bank, to demonstrate against corporatizing
the globe. While I marched with thousands outside,
inside buildings guardsman in riot gear laughed
                                         with politicians,
straightened out each others shirt collars and lapels,
smoothed shirts free of wrinkles,
talked about what the newest gadgets could do to people—
pepper for the eyes, ear-splitting whistles to burst eardrums,
certain kinds of clubs to cripple an attacker,
electrically charged zappers, cattle prods,
laser stun guns—crowd-control tools, he said,
walking outside to join hundreds of guards
lined along the streets,
                             shielded, helmeted, armed riot police,
and soon enough policemen lobbed tear gas canisters
and tried out their new toys as we fled
from sirens, choking from mace and tear gas,
shouting democracy, denounce corporate global greed.

Later, on the way to my hotel I walked past
                     wealthy communities

graveyard quiet,
manacled in surveillance cameras, alarms
barbwire walls, armed mobile-patrols,
triple-lock doors and machine-gun wielding
paramilitary guards roaming paradise
with leashed killer-dogs.

Most of the mansions were owned I supposed
by business millionaires,
drug dealers and corrupt politicians,
crooked investment bankers,
borders guard commanders
on the take,
arms dealers, mercenaries for hire…

I panicked,
my pulse felt like distant gunshots in the night,
and spirals of black smoke rose
from every poor quarter of my heart,
when I realized
we would always have to live with
police searching, seizing and assaulting us.
I'm a peace activist whose door has been splintered
and I've been dragged out
because I no longer will accept their lies,
no longer believe
killing my sons and daughters
is patriotic—
I know the weight of an eighteen-year-old corpse

is worth only as much as the market price
of oil in a drum.

And so I return to my poetry,
refuge from a maddening world,
addicted to violence, money and power.
Poetry thrives in times of war,
survives the bombs,
rough-paw poems that dog-pant
in the rubble, jowl shaking next to bullet-ridden walls,
exuberantly barking among masked faces of resistance fighters.

There'll be other times for poems in the park
amid mothers, infants and soccer players,
tattooed on pregnant women's breasts,
ex-con stomachs, boxer's backs,
on hands of homeless boys and girls
on ghetto steps,
poems blasting from lowriders
cruising on Friday night,
                    but for now let there be
                    sledge hammering poems to
                    crack the stonewall separating Palestinians
                    from Israelis, sledge hammering poems
                    crushing mosques, churches and synagogues
                    where priests, rabbis or ayatollahs would incite hate,
let these poems
move mouth to mouth for peace,
let these poems drown out

the pious babble of patriotic bigotry,
                    and move mouth to mouth,
gas station attendant to the butcher to the truck driver,
mother to daughter and father to son,
roaring peace from cassette tapes,
peace among occupying imperialists and terrorist,
peace between my north and south Chicano brothers and sisters,
peace recited rap-style in high crime areas, peace
to the dreamless crack-smoking children of the night.

1-23-04

Your first cold Esai,
makes you miserable. You didn't sleep at all
last night, nor I nor your mother.
Half asleep, I heard her rise a dozen times,
shift in bed all night
moving from right to left, one side to the other,
whimpering and wheezing,
sometimes crying out loud enough
to spider crack the foundation of the house.

This morning, you were not your usual self—
normally your mother and I lie in bed for an hour,
talking, planning the day, going over yesterday's
events, bringing up issues I don't want to talk about
but which I eventually laugh over,
and laugh even more when you kiss, hug us,
when I hold you upside down by your legs
and swing you like a monkey
when you crawl over my chest pulling my chest hair
as if it were a newfound island of strange herbs.

Yes, a nasty cold,
but it's only the beginning my son.
I tell my woman that you'll
have a good life—two beautiful older brothers
to watch over you, enough money set away
in the bank to take care of your college and travel,
but you won't be able to escape
the cold, the betrayals, the hurt and pain
that awaits you my son.
Tigers, lurking around every turn in the journey,
their claws will tear your heart open
and their powerful jaws will lunge at your throat,
but despite this,
our love for you now, every minute of every day,
strengthens you to rise, to go on,
and realize your dreams, that is what our love today
does for you tomorrow.

＊

The night you were born Esai,
I planted a tree in my heart
to remind me of certain promises I made
to you—one was to always be there for you,
the other to love you,
the other to take care of myself so I could live
a long time with you. I look forward
to playing with you, fishing with you,

waking a thousand times and talking gently
in the morning
                        about your concerns.

The tree I planted has passed through almost four seasons,
now in January, I pick pomegranates
red scintillating seeds mirroring sunlight.
I am fascinated by this fruit,
wonder how God could imagine such a
round, lumpy, scarlet seed fruit,
so hard to get out, to eat in big bites,
one must be patient to nibble the seeds,
pluck them, crunch them with teeth, savor
each delightful little hard-earned seed.

For days now you've wailed
over the pain in your teeth. When you open your
mouth, I see a white ridge beneath your gum line,
teeth, trying to come out. You will have to grow
teeth in other areas too, for instance:
when you don't want to study—teeth to bite down
and grip the books and see it through.
Teeth on your words to say what you mean.
Teeth on your fingers to hold the dream you want
and never let it go.
Teeth to defend your love, your heart, your life.
and the teething in these areas is more painful
than teething your gums,

when the heart grows teeth,
they become roots, and the roots hold you steady
in the fiercest storms.
The tree I planted, has teeth, my son,
molars and buckteeth
to hold the entire universe
in its boughs and leaves,
offered to you as my fruit,
which now blooms with you in your highchair
in the kitchen,
where mother has cut up apple, orange, pear, and banana
wedges you clench with your finger-teeth and munch.

1-25-04

My birthday was January 5th
but I let it go by unnoticed
as I have the other birthdays,

          all clustered
          together in the rain gutter
          like packed in dry cottonwood leaves
          hit by a sudden gust,
          blows them across my view
here in my office, writing, I see the morning
is gray and leaden with dull clouds threatening to rain,
throwing an ashen pallor, shades of various depths and intensity
drape the roads, veil the air, cloak the yards—
I feel as if I am waiting on a man to arrive
or a woman from another country
and she will tell me something
brought from the spirit-world,
that will somersault me from dark depths like the divining rod
shudders over water.

Esai, my sweet child,
NASA's second Mars Rover has landed
safely on Mars this morning,

and over the one hundred twenty-four million
miles tiny molecular bits of energy are soaring
to arrive, like smoke slowly shaping into a photo
of Mars landscape:
a red landscape,
slab and crater bedrock heart,
sizzling into earth's atmosphere
robotic machines unlike our hearts—

          I enjoyed lazily lying in bed
          with you and your mother,
          longer than usual, playing under the blanket games,
          create a cave from blanket game,
          peekaboo under the blanket,
          laughing, snuggling, nuzzling
          we nibbled toast, drank coffee and orange juice
                             in bed,
          read an animal book,

                    no highspeed internet helping us,
                    and moments while you were
                    nursing at your mother's breast,
                    I prayed our world
                    become more peaceful,
that America stop killing Iraqis,
that we leave their people in peace,
that no more crack-head moms
let their children burn in motel fires
while they're out buying crack,
that American prisoners are treated more humanely,

that we stop the insanity of building prisons,
that the man who died days after winning the lottery
be given ample love in heaven,
that our armed service people hated by the world
because our president invaded countries, stole their oil,
come home,

        that they lie in bed
        like me, playing with their infant
        while the woman they love
            caresses their ankles
            under the blankets,
            while their baby laughs
            and giggle-hiccups sweetness
                to his parents
                as mine does to us—
Lord, I pray, let them lay in bed
and play under the covers once again,
fingers sticky with homemade raspberry jelly,
orange juice and coffee,
hands and legs and heads all intermingled
And entwined and braided, running through
each other, against each other
so they feel the three of them are one.

1-26-04

First big snow for you Esai,
although we've driven up to the mountains
where fog and crusty patches of snow
and hoary mist moved across the air
                    like trench-coated phantoms
                    in disagreeable conspiracies
                    hovering secretly in a room,
                    this snow is different.
Stuck to the ground, cold last night,
I can imagine people brought out
slippers, blankets, tea, and put
their favorite video or CD in
                    curled up by the fireplace.
I can imagine—
                    it was a poet's evening last night
                    Esai, for ill-fed dogs and poets
                    because everything crunched in on itself
                    overcast gray sky and air
                    became a brooding prisoner holding trees
                         street lamps, houses,
                         and people
                         hostage, at gunpoint—

and it seemed the grayness and the chilled air
and enough weapons of sadness to blow the
whole world up
and reduce it
                    to a single weeping clown standing
                    over the smoldering rubbish
                    of a carousel merry-go-round
                    with the music still playing
                    the song we all remember as children—
                              but none of this happened.
The sun rose
sparkled like a laughing child with new buckteeth
who can suddenly hear himself utter his first cuss words,

This woman I call the morning dances barefoot in the snow,
                    throwing her bracelets in the trees,
                    showering the air in glittering
                    flakes of light, falling
                              sparks and glints falling.
It is a morning of hope,
our hearts awake to the day
a bird dog sensing a bird in the bush
suddenly stiffens with attention,
turns and points at the asphalt road
leading to a girlfriend's house, leading to a school,
leading back to the home we were born in,
And we leap in the tall grass, across yards and fields,
under street lights, back to the hospital,
to tell someone what we meant or didn't mean,

barking our bone-loving hopes all the way.

Your first snow Esai,
eaves dripping with cold snowmelt,
dogs curled up against the door
where sun hits the warmest,
my thoughts about teaching whittled down
by the brilliance of this snowfall,
leaving my ideas snow puddles gleaming blue
sky and clouds that reflect in them on the patio,
                    and you, divine child,
                    teaching me that the more I do without
                                        in this world,
                    the more I have to give.

1-31-04

Stayed a few days at the Mabel Dodge
Luhan house
                              in Taos,
Maria and Judy gracious and giving,
the way they smile and move and hold
you in their sight,
listening with happiness, listening with dream
listening with hope
with appraisal and inner strength,
with commitment to justice
as a loaf of black bread
sliced and set out on the rough-cut antique wooden table
steams in the cold sunlight streaming through kitchen windows.

I want to say thank you for your hospitality.
Sage incense singes the dawn air
with its pungent aroma
as a shooting star's streak of light
                              on night sky.

I hope our gratitude remains there,
the aromatic afterburn of a shooting-star

filling the rooms with our thankfulness.

During the night,
jammed alongside each other
like sink rags squeezed thin
by scullery fingers, we tossed
and turned and were awakened
by Esai falling out of bed
landing on the floor with a thud—
immediately his mother swooped him up
and his cries turned to whimpers
and milky cluckings at her soothing nipple.

In the middle of the night, you fall out, glide
in dark air,
neither hawk, sparrow, nor crow,
flesh and bone infant,
flying for an instant, flying
remember that Esai, you flew once.

> Earlier that evening
> your mama set some blankets and pillows
> on her side on the floor
> hoping you might
> sleep there a little
> > while we made love—
> > but of course, you didn't
> > agree, but who would know
> > that those same blankets and pillows

                    would break your fall—
We will always plan
on making love,
and wherever you fall my son,
we pray you land
on cushions and blankets.

There in Taos, Esai, you were fluid
creek water streaming in gleaming currents
from arms to arms, until in mine,
I gathered you in the bucket of my arms
and carried you up the stairs
to nap.
You splashed about, your arms and legs
spilling over, uphill a few more steps,
I finally set you down to rest.

As I watched you sleep,
I prayed you leap out of boundaries
and borders and perimeters
society will try to impose on you.
leap out and give yourself
to life, fields, air, the day.

There in Taos,
my voice became calm, the city-edge gone,
my words were slept-in bed linens
muffled bundles of soiled sheets
stripped from orphan beds

on wash day;
your mother's voice was a clean-smelling
sheet fluttering white freeing
from the clothes line,
gliding away on a breezy gust,
over the prairie, foothills and toward the canyons.

And yours Esai, you laughed the whole time,
your laughter was a giant white bird
migrating into our hearts,
settling in on the roads and fences
we set up
to keep us apart from others
settling in and making what we created
to keep others out,
                              but your laughter made it
a bird refuge
where all who are tired from journeying
are welcome to rest.

PART TWO

3-3-04

You learn to walk,
fall on your butt, rise, fall, rise
                              a waterfall
plunging and folding in on itself to the floor
crystalline sparkling roar
over-brimming with life.

                    You touch us all
with your thirst for life, your unending attempts
at walking two steps, three steps, four steps,
indulging happily in your sacred journey
filling yourself up a little at a time with your newly gained skills,
filling me with your lovely walks….
                              I believe
your steps are acts of love against cruise missiles,
you open arms as you rush headlong to me
acts of love against bigots who would label Protesters
                              terrorists,
your hilarious laughter
an act of love against nuclear stockpiles,
each of your penny-sized footsteps describes the true
meaning of Democracy,
and passionately resonates the extraordinary miracle

of our humanity and gentleness—

        I don't know
        how to utter the words that describe
        your beauty as you toddle around the house
        in your pajamas,
but I will tell you
as your mother cuts carrots, mushrooms, adds basil, bay leaves,
potatoes, celery, lentils, onions, garlic, oregano, salt, and broccoli
for a soup,

        and as the sky darkens with sorrowful clouds
        like pages of omens in an epic story,
        somewhere, a tiny jewel spirals
        in water to blue bottomless depths,
        in all of that we observe this day
            the jewel loses itself, turns in
            flashing crescents in descent,
        announcing to the darkness our hope,
        our truth, our beauty,
        our song of our humanity,
our love of peace and people, our love of life,
settling in the sand at the bottom of the ocean
where thousands of men and women back from the Iraq war
limp with plastic legs and hooks for hands—

        they too are blinded by the flash
        of our desire for peace,
handicap dissenters who have at least returned alive,
filled with bits of angry shrapnel,

conscious in their guts that the war was fought for oil rich men
from Texas and CEO gluttons in the Carlisle Group.

This morning my sweet son,
touch the universe with awe in your hands,
touch it for all of those who have no
hands, no fingers,
see for those who have no eyes,
hear for those who have become deaf,
let your heart pound for all of those
who's hearts have silenced in fear—

your powerful love of freedom and justice and equality
can level standing armies,
can bring justice back to the bench,
can protect our rights and homes and families,
can destroy nuclear weapons,
can respect and fulfill treaty obligations to Chicanos
broken by the government, can neutralize chemical weapons—

I don't say this rhetorically,
I believe the power we have as people
can do this.

Money cannot love a person,
a person living a rich way of privileged life
can forget
the wonder of life—
know that darkness is a country my son,

where men and women howl obscenities at each other,
and that as you walk now, in the light of our love,
in this house from room to room,
fortified by your mother's gay laughter
and my brusque, bearish delight,
enjoy these radiant days

           laugh loud so miles away
           they can hear you
           in India and Pakistan,
           so your laughter breaks the bulbs
           lighting the New York Stock Exchange board
           streaming out minuses and pluses on stocks,
           laugh my son even as you walk
           through the darkness of war and racism
           and hate,
           and when you close your eyes to rest,
           believe love is possible, possible with peace,
           love and peace and laughter go together
           like hot soup on a chilly morning.

But for now, continue on with your trying to walk,
a young-born on the prairie
clambering on shaky legs,
toppling over and trembling up again
soon, your hooves and paws and wings will become
fire in the wind....

3-13-04

It's not enough that you have two eyes
to see with, because they will deceive you
with manipulated images,
two legs to walk on are not enough
because they will try to make you march
in the military and occupy a country, invade its streets.

They will try to tell you
if you dissent, if you disagree
if you know the lie is a lie and you
confront the liars,
that you are unpatriotic,
accuse you of being anti-American.

It is not enough that your hands can touch and feel,
grasp and hold and pick up things,
when they try to persuade you to hold a rifle
against a brother or sister in another country,
you must use them instead to embrace and hold and offer.

It is not enough to have a splendid education,
use your ideas to protest nuclear bombs,

despise the cowardly scientists at Los Alamos
manufacturing new ways of killing future generations,
preparing unborn babies' execution in the work they do—

Who are these murderers, these mad men and women?
they work for the World Bank, World Trade Organization,
International Monetary Fund.

        It is not enough to love—
        you must fight them for your freedom,
        retrieve your dignity,
know your voice is to express truth
feared by those who thrive on lies,
know that sincere words
are as trout flailing upstream
        to our birthing waters.

            ☙

I don't have time to take on
politicians every time they lie,
every time they connive
to take, destroy, and steal,
as our mayor (Chavez) and police and politicians do,
        I don't have time stop work,
        ask if I can leave,
        go down to the courthouse
            or police station
                or nuclear waste site
and protest.

They know this.

Built into every work contract
should be a clause allowing workers
to protest when needed. Paid leave (for political protest).

How can we organize if they do their dirty work
when we're working to feed our families?

That's why Esai, and your brothers Tone-B and Gabe,
I buried three cans with money in the back yard,
its your tin can inheritance,
should you ever believe in something
so much you have to leave work
engage your activism full-force,
fight for what you believe,
> go out into the streets and march,
> you can afford to get fired,
> leave work, pick up a placard
> and march in the streets
> with lunches packed, bottles of water full,
> and money in the tin can.

3-14-04

I wonder as I watch my son walk
across the kitchen, pulling cupboard handles,
unsteadily wobbling into the sunroom,
why, if there is so much joy in watching
a child develop into a person with love and compassion,
seeing him mimic my gestures with my hands,
when I cough he coughs, I brush my teeth and he
does the same except he has no teeth,
when I see my child and know there is love there,
there is curiosity about the world,
there is intimacy, how he loves to grab and hug,
smile, laugh, go out as we did the other day
for a long walk along the river banks,
                    why, with all this evidence of our nature,
do my brothers and sister still churn out
robots, small kids intent only making money,
why do Latino parents strive so hard
to make their children lawyers, bankers, engineers—Why?!!
                    —occupations that destroy life,
                    more and more take from life and turn it
                    into a casino,
                    millions of Latino children pushed and urged and forced

                    to become mainstream consumers,
what a terrible waste of life.

I will teach him to draw his dreams out
like a small sparrow, picking up each twig and grass blade
to make his nest where he can rest safely in the branches
of his favorite tree—
                    I want my son
                    to treat each day like a twig or grass blade
                    place his dream in a nest of them, to incubate
                    and allow his heart to break from the shell
                            on its own time,
                            wings spread, the unending skies
                            his boundaries.

3-14-04

This morning Esai's heart is at peace,
he's a rascal, raising up on his feet
to search out and inspect every nook
in the house. I wonder what Esai's reaction
will be, with his heart filled with so much love,
when he sees kids his same age arming themselves
in the streets, kids his same age
shooting up heroin and meth into their veins,
when he sees Chicano kids denying their culture
when we've taught him to be proud of his culture,
when he sees Chicanos beat in the street,
and the wealthy and affluent class of people afraid to murmur
one word of protest?

                        What will he think
                        when standing at the bus stop
                        as he reads how politicians and
                        government authorities
committed horrendous crimes
and the courts let them go free,
when drunks and addicts are gunned down
by hired mercenaries called police,
what will he feel when he realizes that for some people

war is a wonderful investment
to make money,

        that the value of human life
        is measured by the market price—$37.50—
        of a barrel of oil.
will what we've taught him
die on the vine like a withered lilac,
will what we nurtured in him about loving others
turn sour and bitter in him,
will he become a victim of thugs and criminals
wearing suits and driving new cars?

        These are the questions
        I want answers to
        when I'm at his bedside
        and see him sleeping so peacefully.

Latinos are so intent on proving
they are Americans, that they sacrifice their lives
in every war in great numbers—

They give their lives in service as government clerks,
a government that pays for their homes, clothes, schooling,
yet always sees them as inferior, suspect
if they speak Spanish, worse so if they're proud
Chicanos. But you see them everywhere, now
        Latinas
        graduating from colleges and universities
        without the slightest impulse to know the truth

about their culture,
every wisp and tendon in their bodies
yearning to be completely assimilated
and emptied of their culture.
Cadavers
drained of blood,
emptied-soul people without reason to live,
no purpose to breathe,
no mind to think freely,
having forfeited the unique qualities of their culture
and speech and communities
to live as corpses in coffins in cemeteries.

Why do my people do that?
Instead of coming to society offering their contributions
and making society richer for it,
songs, poetry, dance, painting all smudged out
in the name of economic success—
                I've seen them,
                smiling Hispanics in suits and new cars
as empty as pork and bean cans
littered around a campfire.
They bore me,
their opinions lack even the dim hint
of originality,
they believe all the hype newspapers spew—
that other countries are wrong and forced us into war,
that all people in prison are criminals,
that blacks and brown people are inferior,

that people with money and privilege are ordained by God
to rule the poor, that schools should have only white teachers,
that white and black rich people should rule us all,
        they are terrified of their dreams,
        like children, afraid they'll wake up
                in the middle of the night
                and scream at the horror
                their minds have conjured
to keep lying to themselves.

They want me to
betray my culture and history
my sense of decency, and be
a brain-dead writer.
I am supposed to allow
        mainstream consumer society
        to treat me as a child,
        a cute housemaid,
        speak in a little girl voice
        cuddled by the master and mistress of the mansion.
        because they cower under the adult voice,
        the angry Latina voice,
        the proud Latina heart,
but I refuse to submit myself to humiliating obedience,
to be hailed by talk show hosts
who spend ten thousand a week on gym trainers,
to be loved by mainstream America
because my opinions are a barometer
snuggled in the seat of the roller-coaster of public opinion,

pro-war, no guts, no original thinking,
terrified to speak out against injustice,
jump-roping my answers in perfect cadence
to their counting, keep in step,
hop-scotching squares in my little private school girl uniform,
drawn out by war privileged rulers and CEOs,
        then try
        and kneel
        in servility
        to people with money and power
        and gag on my own putrid stench.

Friendly Latina writers call and email me,
want me to be a meal-ticket writer without gumption,
a writer who rallies behind anyone capable of promoting my career,
a writer terrified of criticizing war-mongering generals,
fearful of being labeled unpatriotic.

They want to dress me up in stylish clothing
a Hollywood stage manikin for public praise,
fans will love my dress, my hairstyle, my shoes, my coat,
my writing, filled with trendy fads of the day,
advocating unbridled consumerism, half-time Chicano
on morning talk shows chattering mindless dribble,
arf in tail-wagging submission, conforming
to any lie for a brimming dog bowl,
they urge me to become their birdcage parakeet
trained to peck grains from money-giving hands and not bite—
        Of course, I declined.

3-14-04

Language—
what does it do
to a person to call me
        spic-wetback-alien—
to scapegoat me for their problems—
sixty-million Latinos like myself rounded up
like stray dogs by the INS, on a whim,
whether we are citizens or not, treated like urban rubbish,
what does it mean that three hundred miquiladoras
along the Juarez/El Paso border,
women working in the American factories,
have been murdered and no one seems to care,
that three Latinos were shot in the back of their heads
and no one showed any concern,
        that Oprah can have a
        show on Immigrant stories
        and not one Chicano family is shown,
that she has on her show
the hip-gyrating boogie booty girls
Hollywood loves to showcase for Americans
with big boobs and big butts,
        or the well-bled and drained of conviction

Hispanic starlets,
men with no opinion on anything
except their own looks, their money, their new cars,
what does it mean
that Charlie Rose has a roundtable of experts discussing
diversity rulings the Supreme court handed down
and the talking heads are all black and white,
                    not a single Chicano
                    as if no Chicana women existed,
                    no other minority…
How many more toilets should I clean,
mansion steps sweep,
how many more of your children should I care for,
change their diapers, teach them to speak,
roll them in buggies around the park,
before you treat me with the same respect
you treat your dog?
                    Tell me,
                    Oprah, Charlie Rose, Police hit squads,
                    how can I convince you I am human,
                    besides being your cook, your
                    housemaid, your gardener,
                    I have a right to dignity, to be
                    treated fairly—
                    It's not enough
                    that Chicanos are the number one
                    group in America
                    with the highest death rates in war,
                    the highest drop-out rates, those with

the lowest health care,
the highest arrests and early mortality
rates (killed by police),
exceeding blacks, whites and Indians,
that we kill ourselves off,
is it not enough to tell you we need
attention and respect—
that we Chicanos are Natives,
we come from ancient peoples,
from the Crane People of Seven Caves,
from Atzlan
which is this continent.

Tell me what more I should do,
on spring break you send your college kids
to bed down with our women,
to swagger drunkenly in our streets, using your privilege and money
to buy your sexual indulgence
because our children are starving, homeless, mothers roam
the streets begging for food, but you are only interested in sex,
drugs, liquor, and power.

I've been your slave in your homes, restaurants, gardens, streets,
I've sacrificed thousands of my lives for every one you sacrifice,
and you won't let me in schools, deny me health benefits,
imprison me, steal my land,

                tell me what to do
                because I don't want my children
                to suffer the same racism, the same injustice,

the same poverty as you have me made suffer.
I have two eyes, hands, legs,
a heart, soul and mind, yet you keep treating me like a beast
fit only to serve you, die for you, work for you
for a pittance of what my labor's worth.

                    I am human.

                 My children are human too.

3-15-04

Yesterday, Sunday,
I went to the village cemetery where my grandparents
and father are buried in the middle of the prairie.
When we arrived
a white owl
flew from a tree on the west side
over to the southeast side and perched on a cedar.
When I am dead, I will come back
as a white owl, my grandma told me.
As in life,
I didn't know where they were, like a boy still looking
for his parents, I went down row after row reading headstones.
on the last row I found them—
(where the owl had landed a hour earlier
trying to tell me).
I'd intended to make promises,
make it a ritual and say profound
things to them,
something suddenly opened in me,
a kind of forgiveness harboring itself
in my bone marrow—
I forgave myself, they themselves,

we each other,
a lifting of dark pain
turned over my heart like fresh soil
in which I found myself a child again,
the wholeness of me surfaced
and I felt as a coyote feels in the prairie,
a sparrow feels on a branch,
all of itself,
all of me
in the kitchen, crawling on the floor,
as grandma rolls tortilla balls
rice, beans, and red chili simmering on the wood stove.

My girlfriend
found a ladybug on my father's grave.
It was as if the ladybug's black dotted wings
touched my shoulder like a sword knighting me—
a sign from my father
that caressed my heart like a parental kiss,
offered its hand like a railing of a bridge spanning
a deep canyon with roaring waters,
its small ladybug wings embraced me
swaddled me like a mother
wraps a babe in a blanket from the cold,
and guided me back through my own fears and anger
into a garden in my soul made of a million green leaves.
Home again
I thought as I knelt on the dirt
and spoke aloud to them

as if they were standing next to me nodding
assent and agreeing with my words.

I could feel the prairie breeze on my cheeks and forehead.

Esai sat on the dirt mound, sifted dirt clods,
while I knelt on one knee and talked
how I would come back with flowers,
plant a tree since the one at his headstone was dead,
even joking I'd bring some tequila for him,
maybe a few dollars to get in to a game
if they played billiards wherever he was at.

        I felt their spirits strong,
        their presence palpable as if they had been waiting
        for me to come for decades.
        I buried a book of mine in the dirt
        told my father if he never read a book,
        now was the time
        to do it, it was our story—
        the story told, now the family's destruction could end,
the story of our family's addiction, drunkenness, violence and poverty
had been written, the circle was closed,
and we could move on now.

        My girlfriend cleaned your grave,
        pulled weeds out, raked it smooth with her fingers,
        set rocks in a cross shape on the dirt,
        poured water from the bottles
        over the stones to quench your thirst
        peeled an orange and gave my grandparents and you

each a sweet wedge.

I kept talking to you and my grandparents
as this feeling of forgiveness opened wider and wider
in me a rippling of pain set free, loosened like white blossom
shook from a branch and floating on creek water downstream.

                  I carried my forgiveness in me
                  like a sweet fragrance all day,
                  driving to the pond where I once played
                  other children as I once was carried their rods,
                  others as I was swung on swings,
                  and I placed my infant in a swing
                  and swung him
                  as I was never swung

by a father,
but all was forgiven.

                  We were all a family again
                  and as I drove into the city limits,
                  I felt like a coyote that had gone too far,
                  a coyote far from the prairie.

9-25-10

Here in Sioux Falls, South Dakota

Two Bulls, a Lakota, and I
walk to the banquet four blocks away
and he talks about some Indian writers
that are more popular among whites
than Natives.
Money and fame are more important to them than the people.

I tell him I like Adrian Louis, he nods, doesn't say much
except Adrian is good, speaks from an Indian heart.
He tells me many of the Lakota Medicine Men
were leaders who gave everything away
whatever came their way they shared with the people,
and he includes, you know Lakota means *the people*.

We don't see as well as we once did,
muscles and bones ache more,
our memories are not as sharp
but
the other men we are live and see and think
in our hearts and

are stronger than ever.

He used to be a fighter back in the day,
sober for 18 years,
he's tall and big boned, braids and scars,
like the night sky we walk under
the blue dark streets, the silence of the rain whispers our story
two men in our fifties who have sparred a thousand rounds
with booze and drugs and racism
and walk tonight as champions
down a street in Sioux Falls,
a Chicano and Lakota, owning the night.

Later, Two Bulls sits at my table reserved for writers,
he's an artist, we don't say much,
I go up and talk to the crowd
about Mexican Immigrants,
how my book *A Glass of Water* details two Mexicans coming north
and the horrors they encountered,
I tell how I gave out two hundred copies of my book to the field
                                                                workers
living in camps, north of Hatch, New Mexico,
and how people came up to me in tears
saying yes, yes, yes, that's how it is,
how our lives are, thank you thank you,
and grateful they fill my car with baskets of roasted green chili.

The book sells very well, I tell Two Bulls
as we sit in the hotel hot tub and I notice Two Bulls' chest

carries the scars of the Sundance ceremony.

I imagine such a ceremony brings happiness to a man's heart,
                                        balance and meaning.

I tell him that all my son Esai has to do is walk into a room
and everyone gets happy, everyone feels important and balanced.
He smiles, Esai is a spirit warrior, he says.
And he adds that there is a full moon tonight
a good moon for ceremony.

We say nothing for a long time
and I think how living with Esai truly is
a continuing joy.
Tomorrow morning I leave Sioux Falls
to resume my joyous ceremony of being Esai's father.

9-26-10

Here in my hotel room
I just talked to you on the phone, Esai,
and you were off to play a soccer game. It's
Saturday morning here in Sioux Falls,
I'm about to go downstairs
and sign books for the people
arriving to the book festival.
I told you kick one in for me
but I'm not sure you will.
You're so funny when you play, you go out there on the grass
and pretty much do what you want, the ball goes one way
but if something catches your attention,
say a butterfly or a flower, you head for it
instead of the ball.
So much like me, when I was supposed to be doing my homework
I was always outside as a kid
jumping or rolling in the dirt because I love dirt,
and I wished I could write a poem on dirt
that blew in the wind
or got into my pants cuff or on my cheek and hair.

And you're the same way,

dirt in your clothes,
flowers in your pockets,
stones in your palm,
leaves in the other hand
and you dash into the house or about the day
filled with life's real poems.

So while you play soccer
sometimes running in the opposite direction from your team,
sometimes dancing, doing a handstand or cartwheel
while your team is battling at the opponent's goal to kick the ball in,
you play another game,
of lavishing yourself
in your joyous exuberance of being alive
growing from the dirt
into a wonderful boy-plant.

By the way, I forgot to tell you on the phone
that your name means

the light that shines equally on all things.